ORINDA   C   5

J398.2
Aliki
     The twelve months
                                    6.95

     O R Jun 80

ORINDA   C   5

J398.2   Aliki
             The twelve months: a Greek folktale.
           N.Y.,Greenwillow Books,c1978
             32 p. ill. 6.95

                                        78-003554

THE TWELVE MONTHS

A Greek folktale retold and illustrated by

ALIKI

Greenwillow Books

A Division of William Morrow & Company, Inc., New York

for Socrates, Niko, Yannoula, Eleni
and their families

with thanks to Mary Kyriakoudis

2 3 4 5 6 7 8 9 10
Library of Congress Cataloging in Publication Data
Aliki. The twelve months. Summary: The poor widow who finds good in every month of
the year is rewarded while her complaining rich neighbor receives a jar of snakes.
[1. Folklore—Greece] I. Title. PZ8.1.A43Tw [398.2] 78-3554
ISBN 0-688-80164-1 ISBN 0-688-84164-3 lib. bdg.

THE TWELVE MONTHS

Once upon a time there was a widow who lived in a hut with her five children. No matter how she tried, she could find no work. She had no money to buy them food, and they grew thin and weak.

One day a rich neighbor said to her, "Since you have no work, you may come to my house and bake my bread every Friday."

The widow was happy to do it, and when Friday came, went to her neighbor's house and baked her bread.

The neighbor was pleased with the bread, but she did not pay the widow for her work.

The tired widow went home with whatever dough was still left on her hands. She washed them in clean water, which she boiled into soup. The children ate the soup and were content for a week.

Every Friday the children waited for their mother to come home and make soup from the left-over dough on her hands. They grew healthy and rosy.

But with all their rich food, the neighbor's children
began to grow pale and thin, and their mother could not
understand why.

"How can this be?" the rich woman asked her friend.

"Your children will soon be skin and bones," the friend
replied. "I'm sure the widow carries away their good fortune
to her own children with the left-over dough on her hands."

When the next Friday came, the rich woman made the widow wash all the dough off her hands before she went home. The hungry children cried when they saw their mother's hands were clean.

"Don't cry, my dears," she said. "I will find something for you to eat."

She went from door to door, until at last someone gave her a crust of bread. She soaked the bread in water and divided it among her children.

Then she put them to bed.

For a time the widow watched her children as they slept, thinking all the while how to find food to keep them from starving. At midnight, unable to sleep, she left the house hoping that in the fresh air she might think of a way to save them.

In her grief, she walked and walked.

Suddenly she saw a light high on a hill. She climbed toward it until she came to a tent.

She peered inside and saw twelve young men sitting in a circle. They were busy talking. Hanging from the ceiling above them was a wooden wheel with twelve lighted candles in it.

Three of the men had their shirt collars unbuttoned, and in their hands held fresh grasses and blossoms. Three had their shirt sleeves rolled up, and held sheaves of wheat. Three wore jackets, and held clusters of grapes. The last three sat huddled together in fur wraps.

The men saw that the widow was tired. They asked her to come in and rest, and set food on a table for her to eat. When she had finished, they questioned her about herself.

She told them about her troubled life, but did not complain.

Then a man holding grasses and blossoms asked, "What do you think of the months of the year, of March, April and May? Do you like them?"

"Oh, indeed," the widow answered. "When they come, the mountains and valleys turn green. The earth glows with sweet-smelling spring flowers. The birds sing and farmers sow their seeds. I have no complaint at all about them."

A man with a sheaf of wheat asked, "What about June, July and August?"

"That is a beautiful time," answered the widow. "The summer sun warms the earth, vegetables and fruit ripen. Farmers harvest the wheat they have planted, and everyone is pleased not to have to wear heavy clothes."

"And September, October and November?" asked a man holding grapes.

"Ah, those are the good autumn months when grapes are gathered. They tell us cold weather is coming and that we must prepare for it. We collect wood and sew woolen clothing so that we will be warm when winter comes."

Then a man dressed in furs asked, "And December, January and February—what about them?"

"They are the months that take care of us," said the widow. "The rest of the year, farmers plant and harvest. Winter gives them a rest. It gives the earth a rest, too, and the snow and rain help new seeds to grow. All the months are good, for each has its purpose."

The men were pleased. One who held grapes left the room. In a moment he returned with a large covered jar in his arms. He gave it to the widow and said, "Take this home with you, and raise your children in good health."

The widow thanked the men, and left with the jar.

At daybreak, she reached home. The children were still asleep. Quietly she spread a cloth on the floor and emptied the jar. It was filled with gold pieces.

She cried out in surprise, and her children woke to see the gold gleaming in the new day's sun.

"Now you will have plenty to eat," she said to them. "Wash up, and I will be back soon."

The widow returned with six loaves of bread and some cheese, and they sat eating and laughing until all the food was gone. Then the widow went and bought grain, and took it to the mill to be ground. She prepared dough with the flour and took it to the baker to be baked into bread.

As she was walking home from the bakery with her hot loaves, the rich woman happened to be passing by. "Where did you get the flour for so much bread?" she asked in amazement.

The widow told her everything that had happened. The neighbor's jealousy grew with every word. She decided she too would visit the twelve men who lived in the tent.

That night, after her husband and children were asleep, she left quietly and walked until she found the tent. The twelve men greeted her and asked why she had come.

"I am a poor woman," she said, "and I need help."

They asked her about herself, about her village and her life. She had nothing good to say about anything.

"What about the months of the year? What do you think of them?" asked one of the men.

"One is worse than the other," she replied. "September, October and November bring us cold and sickness. Then come December and January with so much snow there's no going out of doors. And that stupid February is even worse! March, April and May are dreadful, as well. They try to act like winter so we'll have nine months of cold. We can't even sit on our terraces with our coffee.

"June and July roast us and August winds have us coughing without end, and blow away the clothes we hang out to dry. Every month makes our lives miserable."

The men exchanged glances. One who held grapes left the room. He returned with a covered jar and gave it to the woman.

"Go now," he said, "and do as I say. When you are back in your home, lock yourself in a room and open the jar. Be sure you don't open it sooner."

The greedy woman ran all the way home and reached there before daybreak. Everyone was still asleep. She quietly locked herself in a room, laid a cloth on the floor, and uncovered the jar.

Before she knew it, snakes crawled out and ate her up, and that was the end of the selfish woman, her mean words and ugly deeds.

At the widow's home, the children grew healthier
and stronger, and they all lived happily ever after.